Marie Grand

My Journey Through the Valley

Raymond,
To God be all
the glory! Rosemary Calhoun
Love you very much.

My Journey Through the Valley

My Journey

Even though I walk through the darkest valley,
I will fear no evil, for you are with me; your rod and your staff they comfort me.

Psalm 23:4 (NIV)

Rosemary Calhoun

Copyright © 2018 by Rosemary Calhoun.

Library of Congress Control Number:		2018902597
ISBN:	Hardcover	978-1-9845-1197-3
	Softcover	978-1-9845-1198-0
	eBook	978-1-9845-1199-7

All rights reserved. No part of this book may be reproduced or transmitted in any form or by any means, electronic or mechanical, including photocopying, recording, or by any information storage and retrieval system, without permission in writing from the copyright owner.

Scripture quotations marked NIV are taken from the Holy Bible, New International Version®. NIV®. Copyright © 1973, 1978, 1984 by International Bible Society. Used by permission of Zondervan. All rights reserved. [Biblica]

Scripture quotations marked AMP are from The Amplified Bible, Old Testament copyright © 1965, 1987 by the Zondervan Corporation. The Amplified Bible, New Testament copyright © 1954, 1958, 1987 by The Lockman Foundation. Used by permission. All rights reserved.

Scripture taken from the New King James Version®. Copyright © 1982 by Thomas Nelson. Used by permission. All rights reserved.

Any people depicted in stock imagery provided by Getty Images are models, and such images are being used for illustrative purposes only.
Certain stock imagery © Getty Images.

Print information available on the last page.

Rev. date: 03/01/2018

To order additional copies of this book, contact:
Xlibris
1-888-795-4274
www.Xlibris.com
Orders@Xlibris.com
775324

DEDICATION

In memory of my loved ones who have fought the good fight, who have finished the race and kept the faith. (2 Timothy 4:7 NIV) Each of you have taught me that, for me to live is Christ and to die is gain. (Philippians 1:21 NKJV)

TREASURY OF SCRIPTURES OF COMFORT

2 Corinthians 7:6-7

    Psalm 86:17   Psalm 23:1-6 (AMP)

    Isaiah 12:1   Psalm 23

    Isaiah 51:3, 12

    Isaiah 66:12-13

    John 14:16

    John 14:18, 26

    2 Thessalonians 2:16-17

    2 Corinthians 1:5-6

    Psalm 34:2, 6

    Isaiah 40:1

    1 Thessalonians 5:11

    2 Corinthians 1:3-10 (The Message Bible)

CROSS REFERENCE

    Isaiah 40:1   2 Corinthians 7:4   2 Corinthians 7:6

    2 Corinthians 7:7   Isaiah 51:12   Isaiah 66:13

Through the Valley

ACKNOWLEDGEMENTS

TO GOD, MY Father who always cause me to triumph and be victorious no matter what. I thank God for choosing me to pen these words to paper. Thank you God for bringing me through the valley and never leaving nor forsaking me.

I thank God for my husband and I honor him for always being there holding me up. Thank you Walter Calhoun for your unfailing support as you worked to help me finish this assignment.

FAMILY CIRCLE

"For God so love the world that He gave His only begotten son that whosoever believes in Him shall have eternal life."
John 3:16

FAMILY IS LIKE a very large circle of people. People that live everywhere, in different states and some even in different countries. They range from the great ancestor's that you probably never knew but heard talked about often. Then the family that's the closest you have a relationship with, grandmother and grandfather, even great grandparents if you are blessed to have them. Mostly for me and my family it started with Big Poppa and Big Momma. I vaguely remember my great-grandfather. But all the Uncles and Aunts I remember. Only one Uncle but lots of uncles-in-law. Still family. Such an important word – family. One we take so lightly. We use it so loosely never fully comprehending the very depths of that word – family. So precious – family. We all have family – no matter how large or small – we all have a family. Some people have what they call extended family – and that's okay. But God put me in a specific family. A specific group of people that I was born into, raised up in, this family that I was with daily until I married.

A lot of people in family eventually leaves. Some for whatever reason. A disagreement, a dislike, words spoken to and at the wrong time causing feelings of hurt and pain. Then there is that permanent separation. A separation that nothing on this earth can return to you. It's an appointment that each of us has to keep. It's our final destination on this earth because it is by no means the end. It's just the end of this journey as we know. The Bible declares that we will live forever. Not here on this earth physically but spiritually we are going to live forever.

So if you believe that you will live forever. *"But physically there is an appointed time to live and an appointed time to die."* (Ecclesiastes 3:2)

So when our appointed time comes it causes a break in the circle called family. There is an old spiritual song sang by The Mighty Clouds of Joy. I used to hear my mother sing it and when I looked closely I could see she would be crying. I had never really seen my mother cry but that day she was crying because her father had passed away, still as a child I never fully understood the words of that song: "Will the circle be Unbroken." I liked the music and in those days I pretty much liked all spiritual music. I liked all music but that was what we mostly listened to. I liked to sing that song too. But being a child, I didn't understand the words, what the meaning of it implied.

In later years, not too much later because I was about ten or eleven when my grandfather died – then shortly thereafter my grandmother passed away. In my small mind I said Big Momma didn't want to live without "Sweet art." That's what she called him "Sweet art." So she passed away and again I saw my mother and aunts and uncles all crying, heartbroken. I would always hear that song on the radio. It seemed to be one they played regularly. I would sing it even when the radio wasn't on. Then my mother passed away when I was nineteen. I finally had a glimpse of what the song was truly saying.

The words went something like this: "I was standing by the window, on a cold and cloudy day. When I saw that hearse come rolling, rolling to take my mother away. Then I saw that undertaker put my mother in the hearse, I said, "Undertaker," can you please drive slow, for that lady that you carrying is my mother and I hate to see her go. Then I said, will the circle be unbroken in the bye and bye. Will the circle be unbroken?

That song really broke my heart that day because I finally understood to a certain degree, (not fully aware) of the full implications. Just what my nineteen year old mind could comprehend. Whenever I would hear the song again it always saddened me. I still like it though.

Today as I got news once again of a friend going home to glory, I thought about her husband, her children, her sisters and brothers, her family, especially her immediate family. That song began to play in my head and it made me reflect on life and the life of family once again.

After the passing of my mother, there have been numerous other's that have gone on home to glory but I could deal with it. To a certain degree, I did what I could and moved on. It was hurtful and I missed them terribly but I was young and that wasn't my main focus. A lot of deaths occurred when we were overseas or a long ways from home. So I wasn't always there to attend the services. I did return for the passing away of my father. I remember I lived in Anchorage, Alaska at the time. We had a pretty good relationship as far as relationships go whenever a parent is never around all the time. It was okay.

I loved him and he loved me and that was that. I flew down, attended service and returned home. In those days I would tell myself, they (he) lived a good long life. He was eighty two – so he lived a long life. My mother on the hand – she died when she was only fifty, I had a brother that died when he was sixteen, and another when he was seventeen. Didn't understand those because they were young but they were also sick. Had some kind of illness. I was young also so I didn't quite understand. Just knew that I missed them. Missed my mama most of all. That was and still is painful.

Family – the circle of life – broken each time someone dies, no matter the reason. They are no longer here. So to answer the question, will the circle be unbroken in the bye and bye is yes. No matter whether I understood or whether I'm ready to let them go, the circle of family life will be broken when death occurs and one of our loved ones are no longer here.

I take comfort today in the Lord. He is my rock, my sustainer, my comforter, my joy, my peace. He is everything I need.

Even in my darkest hour when I miss my love ones so much it hurts, even when I don't want to do anything but sit around and do nothing. Even when my mind wants to dwell on the ones that have gone. Even when sometimes when I wake up in the morning and just don't even want to put my feet on the floor. Knowing I need to go to the bathroom (smile), even in the midst of all of this, my Father, my Rock, my Lord, and Savior, will have someone to call with an encouraging word or I will ever so clearly hear signs of life outside my bedroom window – the birds chirping (singing), the squirrel's running on top of the house. His creation rejoicing and being glad for another day. That has a way of snapping me out of that mood. Thank you Jesus. He loves me enough not to allow me to stay there in that place of sorrow.

I have to call my friend's husband. He's our friend too. I was lying there praying for the family and I asked the Lord to give me special words of comfort for Him and immediately He said, "I am with Him, I will always be with him, I will never leave him, nor forsake him." "No matter who leaves you, I the Lord am with you. In your most painful, darkest hour, I am with you." That's in Hebrews 13:5b. He also tells us, "Lift up your eyes unto the hills, from whence comes your help. All my help cometh from the Lord, which made heaven and earth." Psalm 121:1-2. God is the only one that can keep you at a time when a loved one passes away.

I have shared many a scripture with friends and families. Lots of time, more times than I care to remember. They always comforted me when I would share with them. It always encouraged me when I shared the Word of the Lord. Some would say thank you, other's would look at me like I had two heads and they were wondering what is she talking about. But mostly the Word of God will and does comfort you if you let it. You have to want to be comforted and consoled. I'm a living witness the Word is able to do that. Not from what I've heard anyone say, I've heard it said lots of times – and it was just words. But there came a time when the Word had to be real for me, to me.

My aunt was ill. Very ill. The diagnosis was not good. I would go and visit her in the hospital, the nursing home, at her house. Wherever she happened to be, I would go visit and give my encouraging words to her and my family (who sometimes looked at me as though I had horns growing out of my head). I would pray with her and for her. She was the oldest relative I had left living. All the others had passed on. So I loved her dearly. She and I didn't always see eye to eye on things. Had some disagreements in my younger days, but God. He knew we would need each other so He fixed me and not only was she my Aunt but we even became friends who could hold a conversation with each other. I loved her dearly. Plus she was the only one left. That stood out in my mind. "She is the only living Aunt."

I remember it was coming up to time for our vacation. The doctor had said there was nothing more they could do literally. I went to see her that morning and she was in a coma. Looking just like I remember my grandmother (her mother) looking. Sorta scared me, anyway I talked to her and sit for a while. No one was there yet from the rest of the family. My husband and I decided to go ahead and go on vacation and that's what we did. Went to Florida. While in Florida visiting with friends I got the phone call I knew would be coming and that I was dreading. Her daughter and my sister called later that night and gave me the news. "Momma's gone," my cousin. Aunt G is gone, my sister. I was taken back. I don't know why, I knew when we left she probably wasn't going to be here when we returned. No matter how you try to prepare for death, you never really can. Even though they told you the person is making the transition you never really grasp that concept even though deep inside you do know. For me it isn't over until God says it's over. He has the final say in my book. Took me back to when my mother passed away. I was very young and very hurt that she was even very sick. They had given the same diagnosis, *"nothing more we can do,"* that really did something to my mind. I was not rooted and grounded in the Lord when my mother passed away. I knew of Him but I did not know Him personally. Especially on that level of trusting and depending on Him. I only knew pain. A pain that is so horrible I wouldn't even go to the hospital anymore to visit my mother. My aunts said it was okay that I didn't want to go. Anyway that horrible call came late one night. All of us was piled in one bed in that old house. There was seven of us. None of us wanted to be alone. Even though they had said there was nothing they could do and she wouldn't live long, I still held on to hope. Maybe they made a mistake. They didn't know everything, but we had sorta told ourselves that "Mama" was dying. As if that made us ready for it. It didn't. When that call came, I knew what they would say. My whole world went black. I thought I was ready because I knew it was coming. I was not ready for that, just like I was not ready for my Aunt to be gone. You can never really prepare for death. Not in the sense of the loss if you know what I mean. Today I have come to understand that death is a part of life. If you live you are going to die.

Anyway my sister and cousin are on the phone. I can hear the sorrow and their crying in their voices. I always believe that no matter what, you should pray. It was definitely time to pray. I told them so and I proceeded to pray. Could only get out a few sentences because I too was so choked up by then. I had gone into the bedroom to take the call. I was sitting on the bed but all I could do was drop to my knees and say, "Oh Lord, Oh Lord." In that moment I heard the Lord say, "I am still God, I am still God." I'm saying to myself, "I know Lord." I know you are God, what do I do with that at this time. My sister and cousin crying on the phone and I can't get any more words out and you telling me I am still God. Okay, I know, now what. I felt like Ezekiel when he asked him these questions about the dry bones, can they live and Ezekiel saying "you know Lord." That's where I was, you know Lord. You know that you are God and I thought I knew that you are God. I just wasn't getting it, but God has a way of helping us out. He began to say that no matter what the circumstance, no matter what happens, where you are, what you're doing, in the midst, "He is still God" and He changes not. He is ready to help you in any situation. If you let Him. I decided to let Him handle my sister, my cousin and myself. That has been very comforting to me throughout the years as I reflect back on "I am still God." It has gotten me out of a lot of tough places as I just remember, "No matter what, He is still God." Circumstances don't change Him, He changes circumstances. He changed my mind. He literally renews my mind as He says in Romans 12:2. Be not conformed to this world but be ye transformed by the renewing of your mind. As He renews my mind, I no longer see things the way I think they ought to be, but I see them the way He says it should be and is. Thank you Jesus for renewing my mind. As I lean more and more on Him, I can do what and how He says to do. Truly Philippians 4:13, tells me: *I can do all things through Christ Jesus.* It's through Him that I have gained an understanding of death. Of life. Of just living day to day. He doesn't want us ignorant of anything and if we are willing the Holy Spirit will teach us all things.

As we go through life, living and learning, we can began to appreciate life and death. Because it is going to happen whether we want it to or not.

The family circle will be broken sooner or later. Death is not something that anyone wants to think of but that doesn't mean it's not coming. We can hide our heads in the sand and pretend all we want to but it is going to happen one day. I'm not saying you should think about death your every waking moment, I am saying you should learn how to let God prepare you for what is going to happen. He does just that. Not so blatantly but subtly, He prepares us for what is going to happen.

As I said, I have shared comforting scriptures with other's numerous times. I have mediated on those scriptures because at the time I really wanted to understand them myself what I was telling someone else. For instance the scripture that says, *"We don't grieve as though we have no hope, for our hope is in Christ Jesus,"* (my paraphrasing). I wanted to know why you have to grieve as though we have no hope. He said, "Because our hope is not in the grieving, it's in Him." Our hope is in Christ Jesus, to comfort us during this time. Our hope is in Christ Jesus as He gives us peace that passes our understanding. Our hope is in Christ Jesus as He gives us joy, unspeakable joy. Our hope is in Christ Jesus because He already bore our grief and carried our sorrow. Isaiah 53:3-4

He is despised and rejected of men; a man of sorrows and acquainted with grief: and we hid as it were our faces from him; He was despised and we esteemed Him not. Surely He hath borne our griefs, and carried our sorrows; yet we did esteem Him stricken smitten of God and afflicted. Because He already did it for us we don't have to do it. I know your heart is saddened. So is mine but I am not going to grieve myself into a state of depression or worse. He already did it for me and for you. Now you have to let Him have it. He said to cast all your cares on Him, for He cares for you. 1 Peter 5:7 Humble yourself in the sight of the Lord, and He shall lift you up. James 4:10. Let Him lift you up.

We have had many relatives to pass and I began to think sometimes of those of us who are still here. My mother had one brother and six sisters. Seven girls including herself. They all had anywhere from 9 children down to one being the least. My mother herself had six children with three adopted children. Out of those six I was second oldest but somehow it seemed like I was the oldest. I guess being a girl, I had those mother tendencies as I had the role of helping everyone else. Especially my three younger siblings. My baby brother was especially needful and he was sort of my responsibility. I took on that role and managed it pretty well. Mama died when I was nineteen so my older brother was twenty one my other siblings ranging in age two years apart. So they were babies when Mama left us.

I was married and lived in Houston, Texas as did my older brother so my siblings became our responsibility. Especially mine. No matter where my husband and I went (we were a military family) they always came and we would spend our summers together. We realized we only had each other. I would always tell them, no matter what, we got each other. We are going to stick together. That's exactly what we did. We grew up, they grew up, got married, had children and life went on. My two baby brothers were still coming everywhere we went so our bond grew closer. No matter where we went in the United States my two younger brothers still always came. I still was the Mama figure in their lives. We fast forward to a day when my husband has done twenty six years in the military, my son is grown and in the military. We retired and live in Houston. Two of my brother's live here. My baby brother in Panama City, Florida. He began to make some bad choices so (Mama) me, I decided (through the guidance of the Holy Spirit) to go get my brother. I did. He lived with us, my husband and I. He got a place and he began to get sick. Dealing with diabetes. Then there came a day when they told me he had congestive heart failure. Wow, that threw me for a loop. Where did that come from? CHF?

I had thought awhile back that none of our families had had a loved one to pass in a while. All of my mama's sister's children were still living. With the exception of three of them. They had children to pass while they were still living.

Bless God, I didn't dwell on the fact that nobody had had death on their side of the family. I counted it a blessing as we were all still here and in reasonably good health. Nobody had any earth shattering illness going on. But things can began to happen really fast.

I remember a cousin passing here. A cousin passing there. Nothing in my immediate world. But I do take notice of things and I do see certain progressions as they take place. One of my elder cousins passed away. Within two or three months one of his son's passed away. Wasn't a year later another son dropped dead? Mind boggling. So hurtful but we move on. It's sort of easy to move on when it's not at your front door.

My sister and baby brother began to battle diabetes. They both began to have complications. They both began to lose limbs. They both began to get worse. So I moved my baby brother in my home and became his care giver. Taking him to doctor's appointments, doing what was needed for him physically and constantly praying for him. By now he is a double amputee. But we dealt with it. Prayer warriors praying and I'm praying. God is so good. He had a couple of times when it became very serious and the doctors were worried. I shared with the family what the doctor said but I always stressed what the Lord says, "He has the final say," is my motto.

Guess I always thought that my brother would always come back home here to the house. I woke one morning with him wheeling through the house saying, "look at my face." It was all swollen. Looked like somebody had beat his face in while he was sleep. I checked his blood pressure, glucose level and it was fine. I called the nurse and she said take him to the hospital so I did. Thinking here we go again. They'll get the fluid off and he'll be home in a few days. A few days turned into a couple of months. Then they moved him from the hospital, to a long term care facility because his oxygen level kept dropping. I had no idea he was so sick. I had just talked to him and he said he was just a little short winded. Well he got worse. Had to be put on a breathing machine. My brother had been there a long time, it seemed to me. Then they were able to turn the machine off him. It was night before Easter. He seemed to be making progress. Easter Sunday I visited as usual and he talked up a storm. My friend came by to visit, and he talked some more. He had had that tube in him and couldn't talk, now you couldn't stop him from talking. I leave, thanking and praising God for the turnaround of his condition. Went for my usual walk on Monday then I get the call from my other baby brother that he is over there and he's non responsive. I'm thinking how can that be, I just talked to him yesterday and he had called this morning. We go downhill from there. My brother doesn't return this time. I call the family. They all come over and we spend the day and half the evening at the facility.

God had warned me. I just didn't want to believe what he said, but he had warned me. Actually shown me that Thursday night. I called my friend and asked her a few questions about faith and another person's will. In her sleepy voice she told me what I already knew. Everyone has a will, you are not out of faith when you say, "your will Lord." Hard pill to swallow. While visiting my brother the next day, the family in the waiting room, I went back and he was having a crisis then. They began to do what they know to do best. They worked really hard. Got that blood pressure down, that heart rate up. It had dropped in the thirties. Even I know what that means. Used to work as a monitor technician in the MICU. Praying, praying, and praying. God is so faithful. One of his nurses said it was good that I was there because that gave him (my brother) the will to live. He is still unresponsive. I go out and share with the others. Don't know what they heard me say but each one had a last visit and they were heading back home to Louisiana. I go see my brother before I head out to go home also. I looked at my brother and I knew, my brother was already gone or as they say, he was transitioning. I talked with him and I felt his skin. It was clammy and wet. I thought it was due to all the medicine they had given him. That really wasn't it. We can almost make ourselves believe anything. Almost. For me, I have to believe God. I have to trust Him. I have nothing else. Only Him. For as He told me with my Aunt, "I am still God." I have to believe just that. I had a talk with my brother. I told him a lot of personal stuff between the two of us. Then I told him, "it's okay Sonny. I know you are tired, if you are ready to go, its okay, I understand."

Sometimes we hold on to people. We cling to them like leeches because we don't want to face what their absence will bring. But a person that's just lying there, has been through the wringer numerous times and now don't know they are in the world, that's not living. We have to know when God is telling us to release our loved ones. That's their right as a believer, we have to release them. That's not part of the life and life more abundantly to be in that state. Trust me, when its time you will know. God will definitely let you know if you really want to know.

I'm not saying it's easy. I'm not saying it doesn't feel like someone ran over you with a Mack truck or an elephant is sitting on your chest. I'm not saying you won't shed enough tears to fill a bathtub. I'm not saying you'll wake up tomorrow (if you can go to sleep) and everything will be back to what we call normal. What's normal anyway? Life, however it unfolds for you is your normalcy.

I am saying, we have a Savior, a Comforter, and a loving Father who tells us, *"I am still God. I am here for you. I can take you through this experience, I will never leave you nor forsake you. Trust me. I am still GOD!"*

When I got that phone call later that night it seemed my whole world stopped. My husband was at work and my baby who was eleven at the time was spending the night with a friend. The phone rang, I looked at the caller ID, wondering what they were calling for never expecting (even though the Lord had told me) the young man to be saying, "Mr. Powe is coding, what do you want us to continue to do." I'm like, what did you say? He tells me again and states how long they have been working with him. He asks do you want them to continue or stop. They work really hard to save lives. I have seen them in action. But I also know, deep in my heart, when to say stop, it's enough. So I said, "Let him go." He said some other stuff that I was not hearing by now. I hung up and called my (natural rock), my niece, who can handle things and get things done even though she doesn't think she can. And she is a praying woman. My sister had not yet made it to Louisiana, so I let her daughter share with her when she got home. Called my husband. He was on his way home anyway. He made it here and the reality of the situation hit me right between my eyes. Sonny is gone. I broke as I fell in my husband's arms. God bless my husband. He didn't know what to do with me. God really did bless him because he spoke to me and I got myself together and began to make calls. Still a functioning nervous wreck. Full of nervous energy. Not all nervous energy because I realized that the Holy Spirit had taken control. I am so thankful I know Him because as I have heard many say, "if it had not been for the Lord on my side, I don't know where I would be." That is so true and I know where I would be if it wasn't for the Lord, don't even have to guess, I would be a stark raving madwoman, but God! Can't say enough how faithful God is. He has proved Himself over and over again. Can't thank Him enough for keeping me in perfect peace, for comforting me when the situation seems hopeless. For strengthening me when flesh just wanted to give in and fall apart. God truly is amazing and He does the amazing. Steps in right on time just when you need Him most. You have to allow Him to be God.

Went through the motion of doing those things you do when a love one goes to be with the Lord. People come and go. You function though you may not want to. People are extra kind during this time. Why can't we be this way with each other all the time? Anyway, thanks to everyone for all they do and did to make it a smooth transition. It could have been a trying difficult time but the prayers of the righteous really does avail much. Experienced that. Didn't know that I could actually feel in the Spirit the comfort of those prayer's and comfort from others. Outstanding!

I really learned how powerful prayer is. I've always believed in prayer, always prayed (for myself and others) had many prayer's answered but this was different. Never had a brother (from my mother) to die, especially my baby brother. Lord Jesus, you've got to help me. This is a tough one.

Our son came, he was a real comfort to me. He kept asking, "mom you alright." Yes, all is well, my answer. He was trying to deal with the loss himself. This was Uncle Sonny who wasn't just uncle but could also be big brother, so I know it was hard for him. God was and is faithful to all of us. He supplies our every need as He comforts us.

We did what we had to do, God did what he does best and we move forward. There is no staying there in that one place, life goes on, whether you participate or not. It doesn't stop because a part of it has changed but it goes on. Just as the world doesn't stop turning, it continues to turn and so do you. We move on because things began to continue to happen.

Just want to say that when we say we are praying for someone, let's just do that and we ourselves believe that what we are praying for is actually taking place. A few well-wishers told me, I'm praying for you. Yet when they saw me, it was as if they expected me to fall out, scream, and yell or some such nonsense emotions. I said you're praying for me (us) right? They say yes, I said, okay its working. Your prayers are working that's why I can rejoice and be glad. That's why I can truly give God the praise and all the glory, that's why I can truly say "thank you Lord." Because of the prayer's. Prayer is powerful. So don't disbelieve what you ask of God. Continue to trust Him that if you ask, He does. It's all Him and none of us. Glory to God!

Got through that ordeal. You try to move on and regain some kind of order in your life. When everyone is gone and it's just you and your memories. I thank God again for being God. He already knows you need Him and He is always there. Have to lean and depend and trust Him more than ever.

Talked to one of my sister's, found out she had to have major heart surgery. Went and stayed with her and trusted God for her healing. He was faithful as He always is. She came through fine. All went well and she is on the road to recovery. Got a call from my oldest brother and Bless God, he is having a crisis. Talked with his family (Linda and Yvette). They gave me a little of what they knew but not much understanding. I arrived home from Louisiana and went straight to the hospital to find my brother hardly breathing. They put him on the ventilator to help him breathe easier and, they began to run test. They had already suspected he may have cancer.

I am a believer. Nothing is too hard for my God. He can do anything. At the name of Jesus every knee must bow, including cancer. That's what I shared with my sister-in-law, nieces, my sister's and my brother's. We either gone believe God or the report we get. I choose to believe God. My brother would be healed of cancer and become a living testimony. That's exactly what he did, he became a living testimony for God. Everything they said they couldn't do, I would tell them that God has the final say. I hear what the doctors are saying but I also know what God is saying and it isn't over till God says it's over. I know that some people will say and think that being on a respirator, being in a nursing facility and not being up running around like you did before is not living. I respect your thoughts but I trust God because He said, *"For my thoughts are not your thoughts, neither are your ways my ways saith the Lord. For as the heavens are higher than the earth, so are my ways higher than your ways, and my thoughts than your thoughts." Isaiah 55:8-9.* I choose to believe Him. As long as there is breath in the body, I choose to believe the Word of God. I got nothing else. So I have to believe God when He says, "We shall live and not die to declare the works of the Lord."

As I said, live and declare the works of the Lord, my brother Robert did. Each day was a new, fresh revelation of the power of God. It was God keeping him here, not some machine. Don't get me wrong, I know God uses natural things in the earth realm but ultimately it's God.

My brother had what is called a DNR (do not resuscitate) order. We went along with it because they said there was nothing they could do. But God showed us all. He began to improve day by day. Nothing drastic but more than they hoped for. He was doing so well, I talked it over with my sister-in-law Linda and asked her if we shouldn't remove that order. She thought so too, so we removed the DNR. He continued to improve. He continued to impact the lives of the people who cared for him and even some of the other residents. Sometimes we don't see God using and impacting other's lives with our lives but He does. There is a reason for everything that happens and for every place that you go. You are there for a reason. Stop trying to get away so fast sometimes and just ask God, "why am I here?" "What would you have for me to do, or even, what do I need to learn in this situation?" There is always a reason for you being where you are when you are where ever you are. I learned to just ask God what He wants me to do or even to say. I know that God had my brother in that place for a reason, had me going out there every other day for a reason and I was alright with that. Not only was I seeing my brother but I got the opportunity to pray for others, to smile and make someone's day, to say a kind word to someone. We never know how we are impacting someone's life just by being in their presence and letting the love of God shed abroad to others.

God is something else. Can't say enough how awesome He is. He amazes me daily. I'm always in expectation of Him showing Himself mighty in every situation.

Well, God used my brother until he took him home. Usually I would make the drive to Katy every other day. I live in Humble, Texas, and Linda in Houston. I would pick her up and we'd go together. Sometimes Walter would go. We would go and he would be doing well. We stayed our usual time (trying to not get caught in that evening traffic). For some reason I called Linda the next morning and asked if she wanted to go and she said yes. Even Walter said he would go, so we headed out. Made it there he was sitting up in the sitting area, all cleaned up and a fresh haircut, (we had teased him the day before about his hair being so long, so he had a fresh hair cut). I asked how he was doing and we were sitting down for our usual visit. He said he was alright, just hungry (he was always hungry, let him tell it). I touched his forehead and it was soaking wet, but cold. So I touched his shoulder and realized that his clothes were wet too. He was sweating profusely. I called the nurse over and she began to check him out. Said, she needed to take him back to the room to run some test, so we followed. Still didn't think anything out of the norm, he was still talking and all. She said his oxygen was a little low, so they gave him a breathing treatment. Still it was steady dropping and they asked us to wait outside. They worked and medicated and did what they could do. Still I'm thinking all is well, they'll get his oxygen level back up. I was wrong. He was leaving us and leaving fast. They said there was nothing more they could do, they were transporting him to the hospital. They tried to stabilize him before they took him out but he was already gone. Yet they worked diligently and took him to the hospital. When we were about to leave the nursing facility I knew in my heart he was gone. His head nurse was saying how sorry she was, so I began to console her. God is so strategic, He had me ministering to her while they had taking him out. Linda and Walter were already in the truck but I was consoling the nurse. She was crying so hard and she really wouldn't let me go. I shared some word with her, got her a little calm, left the parting words that "God has the final say." She was a beautiful person and I thank God for allowing us to touch each other's lives.

We made it to the hospital where they showed us to a special room (where you know if something has happened, this is where they put family). We didn't have to wait long before the doctor came in and told us what I already knew. My brother was gone. Another brother gone. It can't be, we just buried Sonny a year and some months ago. Was it even that long? I really don't know. We had throughout the past month, laid Linda's mother to rest, then a few months later, her brother and now almost a year to date her husband. My Lord. Help Jesus. That's all I had at the moment. Jesus! Linda broke, I think I cried out, my husband sat there stunned. The doctor still trying to tell us all they had tried to do. Whenever there is a crisis, I open my mouth and out flows tongues. That's all I got. That's all I can do until the Holy Spirit calms me and I allow Him to take control.

It doesn't matter that you know someone is gone, when they officially tell you, it knocks the wind out of you, drain you of all emotions (for they, your emotions) are all over the place. Tears your heart into pieces and makes it hard for you to breathe, let alone think. But I am like the Weeble (a toy punching bag that came out when our son was a baby, a great toy). You would punch it and it would wobble over to a certain degree but then it would wobble back up. The slogan was, "Weebles wobble, but they don't fall down." Great toy. I'm like that, we as Christians are like that, we get punched and wobble but because we are rooted and grounded in Christ we don't fall down. In the bottom of the weeble is a weight that keeps it from just falling down and staying down. It has to wobble back up, so do we. Christ will not let us be consumed with grief, pain, sickness, disease, or whatever, He is the solid rock that we are weighted in and we are rooted and grounded in His Word which causes us to triumph in every situation. Even the death of a loved one.

So many people that I knew were dying and God showed me that death is a part of life.

It's a part we don't like, a part we don't want to deal with but it's a part that we can't get away from. For as sure as you live you will die. Scripture says it is appointed unto man once to die and then the judgement. Hebrews 9:27. So there is an appointment with death that we all have to keep. It's the order of God. But we don't despair nor are we discouraged. God has a plan and we follow and carry out His perfect plan.

We composed ourselves, as best we could and called the rest of the family, and, for me once again, I cried, "Jesus, Jesus, Jesus, I need you like never before. Once again I'm glad my husband, my friend, my rock here on earth (Walter) was by my side as always. So grateful to God for that man. He doesn't say much but when he does it's what is needed. Thank you Jesus for Walter. Thank you Walter for always being there.

You know, during times like these there is no use questioning God or letting your mind wonder here and there about what if's, what and's, and what could have been's. Just ain't no use putting yourself through that. Let the Holy Spirit do what He does best, take control of you and lead and direct you in what needs to be done.

We called the family after we had sort of composed ourselves if you can call that being composed. Each call was a challenge within itself. Telling someone their loved one has passed away is never a pleasant task. No easy way to do it either. But once again, you do what has to be done. By now you are going through the motions, you make decisions, you are in that place where nothing seems real anymore. You're dreaming and will wake from the nightmare. Unfortunately its not a dream. It's time to go home. The calls began to come in, you laugh, you cry, you eat, you can't believe what has happened. Your physical body is tired but sleep is a million miles away. You want something but you just don't know what it is. There is nothing more to do today. You are in that unreal place of unbelief. Maybe hoping a mistake has been made, but you really do know it's not a mistake. Especially when you call the funeral home for them to pick up the body and they give you a time to come in and make arrangements. Once again, making arrangements.

I only had to help this time. No critical decisions for me to make. Just help my sister-in-law and her children make it through this time as peaceably as possible.

The funeral home staff is some of the kindest people I have come in contact with. I know it's their job, but this funeral home has a real special and caring environment. Makes you feel like family. That they loved your loved ones as much as you did. They did an excellent job. They exceeded all my expectations and more. Thanks so much to them for a job well done.

My brother used to tell me "when I die, I want you to do this and make sure you do this, "I would tell him, I'm not doing nothing." I'm just gone be there for Linda, I would laugh at him and ask what are you going to do if I go before you. He would say, "Romary, (never say my name right) just do what I ask you. Then we would laugh cause I would still say, I'm just gone help Linda." And that's what I did. I tried to be there for her and do whatever she wanted done.

I felt so bad for her. Her mother, then her brother, and now her husband. Lord Jesus. I know how I felt about my brother but my heart hurts for her. But, God is faithful. He carried our sorrows and bore our pain once again.

We had a beautiful ceremony for Mr. Smith (my brother). I always called him Mr. Smith. I miss him so very much already. I didn't stay in that mood very long though because I went to visit our son for the summer. That really did help me with the transition.

I had been used to going to the hospital, nursing home every other day and now I had nowhere to go and nothing to do. Nothing that I really wanted to do. So it was good in a couple of weeks of laying my brother to rest, I went away on vacation. That helped me a whole lot. Even though I missed him and Sonny terribly, being away really did help. I had a whole new daily routine and it was one I could deal with.

Our son would ask, "Mom are you okay? Yeah, I'm better than ever." He would then say, "you know Mom it's the strong people that people forget to ask how they are." I would respond, "I really am okay." I can truly say that I was okay because I knew that God had me. He still said, "I know Mom, but are you really okay?" I had to explain to him that yes, I really am okay. If I stay over here in the Spirit and trust God, all is well, because God makes it so. But, if I come over here in the natural, I can't tell you how I would be, so I'm just gone stay over here with Jesus and let him keep me. I thought about the scripture that say: "Walk in the Spirit that you may not fulfill the lust of the flesh." So I decided through the power of the Holy Ghost, I'm going to stay over here with Jesus. He's all I got. That's what I did, what I am doing and what I am going to continue to do. I can't sit around twirling my thumbs and wishing for something that isn't going to happen. As I said earlier, life goes on. You can go with it and be productive or you can stay where you are and become stagnant. That's not life and life more abundant, not for me anyway.

God is bigger and better than that. Remember I said, He has a plan. He does and it doesn't stop when interruptions come. Interruptions, like death, are a part of life. Put them in the proper perspective and let's move on. Keep it moving if you can?

I miss my brothers terribly. Sometimes it's overwhelming (the missing their phone calls and visits). We talked every day and now no talking to them. No getting together with them. Thank God for my other sister's and brother's. That always helps. Talking to the others, doing stuff, just keeping busy. Just trusting God. Very important. Quite time with God.

There was a time in my walk with God early in my Christian life. I felt as though I was just going through the motion. Nothing happening, just routine, every day stuff. I would visit the sick, volunteer at the church, attend all kinds of conferences and spend time with Christian friends. Always something going on. But I just felt like something was missing or I needed to be doing something more. Just feeling because I really did have a full schedule. A friend asked how's it going Rose and I would say, "Oh, nothing much." She would always ask and my response would always be the same. Even though I thought there should be more, it was a time of rest and little did I know it of great peace. I finally told my friend one day that it seems as if nothing is happening in my life. Just moving right along from day to day. I should have just been thankful. She said, "Rose, if nothing is going on, you better just enjoy the rest, the peace, the calm. I really didn't understand what she meant at the time, but I do now. Life started moving like a Ferris wheel and it hasn't stopped. Don't get me wrong, I have made the transition as it is required but those days of nothing happening in my life, are long gone. Things started happening and hasn't stopped. To God be the glory though, because He has bought me through each challenge. I'm a better person for the experience and most of all I have had to learn to trust in the Lord with all my heart, to lean not to my own understanding (that always got me in a place I didn't want or need to be), to acknowledge Him in everything (no matter how seemingly minute), acknowledge Him, ask Him, and He has never failed me. Even when my understanding wasn't where it needed to be or I couldn't see how it is going to work, I had to trust God. I've always believed what the Word of God says and I am always telling others, "the Word of God says." It's easy to say that. Putting it into action is another thing. Situations and challenges will cause you to learn or else. I choose to trust the Word of God. He's the only one that I know who never lied, cheated, killed, hurt or anything else. He is what His Word declares that He is and He's faithful in all His ways. He can be trusted because He cannot lie, He is truth. His Word says that He is the way, the truth and the life. I find that to be true in my life and I've seen it come to pass in the life of others. So I have no choice but to trust Him. Most of all I have no choice but to obey Him. He always come through for me, that's why I can truly say, I am better than ever, for He makes it possible for me to be the best I can be in whatever I do.

Again, God is so strategic in all that He does. There was a time when I was in a situation and was tired of being in it. It had been a couple of years and I just wanted it to be over with and on to the next assignment. No matter what I wanted, that wasn't God's plan. I even prayed and shared with God that I would learn whatever the lesson was He wanted me to learn if He just ended what I was in. I was always in a hurry. Always on my schedule and not God's. I even would say, "I'm not going before God, He has to go first." Then I would turn right around and get ahead of God. Well this day, God spoke to me loud and clear. I said, "God I'll learn the lesson." (Since I believe things that happen, happen for a reason and there is always a lesson to be learned) The Lord spoke clearly and said, "I know you'll learn the lesson, you just won't learn it the way I want you to." I was so taken back. I thought about arguing with God that I would and realized He is right. (He is always right). That opened my eyes and caused me to re-evaluate the situation I was in and to humbly ask God what He wanted me to learn in this situation. I realized and learned in the days and months to come, I needed to do some growing in a lot of areas and this lesson was just what I needed to help me learn. I learned not to always be in a rush to do things. To take the time and pray and see what the Lord was saying about it and how to handle it. I could grab a hold of something and be off and running. Nothing wrong with that but was that what God wanted. I was very impatient. Also very short fused with God's people. I needed to slow down, appreciate where I was at the time and learn from whatever was going on and not try to solve and have a solution for everything and everybody. I had to learn to listen and hear what was being said and then meditate on what God wanted me to hear and not what I thought I heard.

I could go a mile a minute and not get anywhere. I had to learn to see God's people as He saw them and love them as He loves them. I am so much better in that area now but I know it was a work for God. I was used to doing things my way and I knew what was best. So I thought. As I studied the Word, listened to Christian television, and listened to different ministers or whoever spoke the Word, I began to allow God to renew my mind. I began to realize that I could not be conformed to this world (do things I had learned in the world) but I had to allow myself to be transformed by the renewing of my mind. *Romans 12:2* I had to allow the Holy Spirit to teach me how to do and think the way the Lord wants it done.

David was a great man of God. The Bible declares He was a man after God's own heart. David also was a man of war. Fought many a battle and won them through the grace of God. He wanted to build a house for the Lord. You would think that is a great, noble thing to do, right, and it is. To do something to honor God and a place where you could go and worship besides the tent that was used as the tabernacle. Great idea. But God said no, you will not build me a house you have been a man of war, and has shed blood. (1 Chronicles 28:2-6) I always thought that was a good thing and it wasn't wrong for David to want to build it, but, God had other plans. If it's not the plan that God has designed it is not a good plan, according to God. And we always want to do it according to the plan of God. *Scripture declares that there is a way that seems right unto man but the end there of are the ways of death* (Proverbs 16:25). Also another one that says, except the Lord build the house, they that labor, labor in vain. So I've learned I need to seek God first. He knows how He wants it done, how it's going to work and the finished product. He said, *"His thoughts are not my thoughts and His ways are higher than my thoughts."* He is omnipresent (everywhere at all times), omniscient (all knowing), omnipotent (all powerful). So with that being said, I need to conform to the Word of God and do what He is calling me to do. Let Him lead me in all truths.

With that being said, I had a few months of rest and relaxation at my son's home before coming home and facing the next challenge.

My very good friend and mother figure whom I had known since I came to Houston to live, was having a health challenge. That kept me pretty busy, visiting her and doing whatever I could for her and her husband. My baby sister also began to have a health challenge. My sister was a double amputee and was now having circulation problems in one of her legs. So here I go again. Doing whatever I could, hospital, home, hospital, back home, again. Neither of them was getting any better. My sister had to be hospitalized and they were trying to see how much circulation there was. There was a bad sore on her stump that just wasn't healing. No circulation in that part of the leg. It was below the knee but, still no circulation. On top of that, she developed infection in her body. Had to stay in the hospital for IV antibiotics. My sister was not a happy camper. She endured though. Her daughter that lived here visited her all during the day and night and I would visit in the daytime. She needed a lot of care. They did a procedures and gave us hope that they could get the infection under control.

When a love one or anyone is having a health challenge it is very important to know what you believe and who you believe in. A lot of people will say they are praying for you and the family and then you hear them tell someone your loved one is dying. "Girl, they said it don't look good!" Makes you wonder, who are these people and what prayers are they praying and who are they praying to? It makes it more of a challenge when you have to fight different spirits as you are standing in faith. All those lying spirits, spirits of deception, spirits of anger, and especially the spirit of death. It is really a faith fight and you better know who you believe in and what you believe. The Word of God declares "be it unto you according to your faith." Thank God for the prayers of the righteous. The Word says those prayer's availeth much.

Anyway, we fight, knowing that as in 2 Cor. 10:4, we don't fight against flesh and blood for the weapons of our warfare is not carnal, but our weapons are mighty through God to the pulling down of strongholds. Eph. 6:11-12, declares, we wrestle not against flesh and blood but against principalities, against powers, against the rulers of the darkness of this world, against spiritual wickedness in high places. We are told to put on the whole armor of God. Why, that we may be able to stand against the wiles of the devil. Know that the enemy comes to kill, steal and destroy. God has equipped us with His Word, with His truth, His righteousness, His gospel of the peace, His faith, His salvation and He has given us a prayer language. So we fight the good fight of faith on our knees.

God had given us the victory and no word curse and other lying spirit's can change that. No matter the diagnosis, we have to believe what the Word of God says. We have to stand on the Word, declare and confess (speak) the Word. It has to be the first thing that comes out of our mouth. Say what you believe and trust God to bring it to pass. You cannot, say one moment, that God is a healer and the next minute declare your head is killing you. God tells us not to be double-minded but have faith in God, not wavering. He says a double-minded man is unstable in all his ways and let him not think that he will receive anything of the Lord. (James 1:6-8) You must act in faith and speak what the Word of God says about the situation. I hear what doctor's and people say and it's probably facts as they know them but, there is only one truth and that's the Word of God. He say we shall know the truth and the truth will set you free. (John 8:32) Learn the truth in God's Word.

You have to study and meditate on what the Word says before you can act on it, before you can declare it. How can you do something if you know nothing about it? You must read, study, meditate, spend time with God, become the Word. We walk by faith and not by sight. So when we hear negative reports or negative statements about that which we know better, we need to denounce it. Send it to the pits of hell. Call it null and void. We don't have to receive it. If it's not in line with what God is saying, I don't have to receive it. It's not over until God says it's over. So we fight the good fight of faith and are not moved by what we see but what we believe.

Very tiring, fighting different spirits and word curses, but thanks be to God, His grace is sufficient. When we have done all we can do to stand, we are told to stand! If He tells us to stand, I just believe He will give me the strength to do it and He will hold me up with His mighty hand. And Amen.

Got a bad report from the doctor. My sister had gone home and had to return back to the hospital. This time to a different facility. Went there and they were going to try something different. With the infection in that leg and no circulation, it was very painful. I prayed for my sister, with my sister and had every prayer warrior and my church praying for her. God is still so faithful. They kept her heavily sedated because the pain was so great. They decided to do another procedure to see just how much circulation there was and maybe they could reroute some arteries or something just to get some circulation. They were really kind and was doing all they knew to do. They took her in to surgery. My niece went to work, coming back when it was over. I waited in the waiting room. No one there but the Lord and I. I prayed and believed God that all is well. The doctor finally comes out after three or four hours. They had said maybe forty-five minutes. I think that's what I remember, not too clear on the time frame, except it was longer than they said. I thought, "They are finding a way and getting her all fixed up. Thank you Jesus. Doctor finally comes out, sit down as if she is literally drained and she was, poor thing. It takes something out of you to tell someone there is nothing that can be done for your loved one and they are going to die. I know that has to be hard for them because they are in the business of saving lives, not pronouncing death sentences. She shared that shocking news and through my fog-filled mind are a million questions. She tried to answer each one as gently as she could but there is no gentle way to say you are going to die and very soon. Nothing we can do but make you comfortable. I asked are you sure there is nothing else that can be done. She is almost in tears as she says no. There is nothing more we can do. I ask what next? She explained they would make her as comfortable as possible, place her in hospice. (I always think of death when I hear the word hospice) Still, God has the final say. I go to the room and she is heavily sedated, out cold. Not a care in the world. They said she probably wouldn't wake up till morning. I called Walter, told him I would stay a few more hours and then head home. Always like to try and beat the evening rush hour, or should I say rush-jam. I talked to my niece. They had called her. Tried to explain what they said to her. I think she got a different report but I told her what I had been told. Thanked God for the doctors and staff and headed home. I think I cried half-way home. I told God, "you know I can't see with this water in my eyes." Still in my heart, I know that God has the final say and it ain't over 'til He says it's over. He makes all things possible, even impossible things.

I come home and call the rest of the family. My sister's and only brother now. I share with them as I had the previous two times what the report was and as always I ask, "Whose report are you going to believe?" I know what the earthly doctors said, but I also know Dr. Jesus had not spoken yet. So they could choose to believe whichever report they wanted to, I know what I chose to believe.

I have never been a negative person. I always see that God can and will do the impossible. His Word declares it and He said He watches over His word to perform it. My brothers and sisters probably thought "She's a little crazy," and that's okay. Everyone doesn't believe the same and that's okay too. Told you I have to stay over here in the Spirit realm with my Rock, Jesus. He gives me the strength when I'm weak, the courage when fear tries to take over, and the peace when worry tries to come in and even joy in my saddest hour. He is that kind of God to me.

They received what I told them and the ones in Louisiana decided to come over and visit. She was in a lot of pain, I mean pain that is indescribable. I would pray and rub her down with oil and quote the Word over her. I never did tell her what they said. Maybe they did or maybe her daughter did but I know she knew what they had said. Seems as if she just accepted it. They kept her drugged up.

They set up hospice care for her to go home. She wanted to go home so home we went. I thank God for the time He gave me with my sister. I am so thankful for how he kept me during this time once again. Thanksgiving was coming up and we were going to all have Thanksgiving dinner with her. The Saturday we planned to have it is the very day she transitioned home to be with the Lord.

They had all come over again, her children and other family members. I had spent Thursday night with her and her daughter. (She was at her daughter's home) Her other children came Friday, so I got a little rest and was going to head over early next morning. Had talked to them back and forth on the phone checking on her. She is transitioning the nurse reported. Saturday morning, I'm getting ready and got the call to come, she is leaving. I say okay and continue to get ready. Seems as if I am moving in slow motion by now. On my way there, I get the call, she is gone. My baby sister is gone home to be with the Lord.

Dazed, I continued on to South Houston. Thank you God for being with me. If it had not been for God I would not have made it, but God. I think Walter was working, Josh was with me and my brother Raymond was on his way to Arizona for Thanksgiving holiday. I told his wife not to tell him until he made it there. He had been having a health challenge and needed the vacation badly. I explained to his wife and she agreed.

So sad when one leaves but also a beautiful thing. It's beautiful because the Word declares that to be absent in this body is to be present with the Lord. And the suffering on this side has ended. No more pain, no more sleeplessness. Horrible, unimaginable pain, even with medication. Even though it hurts terribly there is a part of me that is rejoicing with her, for the battle is over for her. God has healed her totally. He didn't heal her the way I wanted but He healed her and allowed her to come home. That was her choice and I respect that. I don't pretend to understand all of this, I'm just grateful to know that God has me and He continues to keep me in all my ways and situations.

We make the necessary calls, just try to comfort each other as other's come in. Really heartbreaking, but, once again, But God." For me it's as though once again I'm having this same dream but with different family member's. These are the children of my sister and her grandchildren and friends. My other siblings of course but it was different this time.

This time seems as if I am doing a lot of comforting. Scripture tells us to comfort one another in 1 Thess. 4:18 and to edify one another. To build each other up. It's something about comforting someone else, you can't stay in that place yourself if you are speaking words of faith and encouragement to others. Not if you mean what you say. Those same words apply to you, therefore you can't stay in the spirit of grief. The Holy Ghost is awesome. He takes over and gives comfort like no other. As Isaiah 61:3 declares, "He, the Spirit of God has been sent to console those who mourn in Zion, to give beauty for ashes, the oil of joy for mourning and the garment of praise for the spirit of heaviness." You do not have to stay in that place of brokenness, of grieving as though you have no hope, as though you don't know what to do next, how can I go on and just all of the negative aspects of death. Don't stay over there! Allow God and those He sends to comfort you at this time to comfort you. It hurts but it doesn't have to break you and cause you to think you can't go on.

You can and you will go on. That's life and you have a choice of how you choose to live it. God is there for you. I can't stress enough, "He said, He will never leave you nor forsake you." You can choose to believe God or what you perceive is the truth. God does what He says and that's the bottom line, the last line. God is always faithful. You can choose to have a pity party and dwell on stuff that will cause you to sink deep into despair and before you know it, you will be consumed by depression. Or you can choose to exercise your faith and trust an Almighty God that wants only the best for you. You can dwell on all the, "why my loved ones," or "why now," or "why did this happen to me?" or why? why? why? There will always be why's. It's how you choose to seek an answer. Nothing wrong with advice from other people, just make sure they are giving you the Word of God and not just their experience. The Word of God is the only true comfort during this time. And sometimes it will feel in the flesh that it is only words. But read it again. Read it again. Began to mediate on what it is saying and let God speak to you. It's so comforting when the Spirit reveals to you what God is saying at this time.

People will share their experiences with you, tell you their "formula" for getting through it, tell you their life story which you really don't want to hear (and shouldn't have to at this time). They mean well and sometimes they don't know what to say or do. And that's okay. It's okay to say nothing, it's okay to do nothing. Everyone's experience is different and we deal with it differently. So let's remember sometimes the best way to help and comfort is just your presence. Just being there with someone and helping as they ask you and provide what is needed. The choice is yours. Let God help you. He is willing and able to carry you through this time. So when God sends us to comfort someone, let's remember we're there to minister to someone else, to help meet their needs. Be led by the Spirit on how to minister at the time. Listen to His guidance and He will direct you on what to say and what to do. Let's not take them down memory lane of our grief. It's not our time. It's another person's and sometimes it's okay to just be quite. Just listen. That can be the greatest comfort of all. Just listen to them can be a great comfort. Me, personally, I don't remember half of what was said to me anyway. Most people don't even remember half the people that come and go. Some people I remember and some I don't. So all I'm saying is, let's just be mindful of what we say and do when we go to comfort someone.

We move on once again, life goes on. Preparations must be made and carried out. That can help during this time. Staying busy helps a lot. There is always something to do. So allow the Holy Spirit to comfort those who mourn and provide solace for those who grieve bestowing on them a crown of beauty instead of ashes, the oil of gladness instead of mourning, and a garment of praise instead of a spirit of despair. (Isaiah 61:2-3) This is a relevant biblical promise for those who are hurting (no matter what the reason). Meditate on this promise and let it comfort you.

We had a beautiful home going celebration for my sister. Just as she would have wanted. Just as she would have done for someone else. My sister was always rising up to help someone, to give of her finances, as well as her time. It was beauty in that, the same thing she made happen for someone else, the Lord allowed people to make happen for her. Such a blessing. Everyone was so kind and giving, just as it should be. I think we should be this way with each other all the time, not just when something happens. Oh well…..

I had a younger brother to pass away in the eighties. After the service, my older brother asked, what now? What do I do now? Later in life, he asked the same question when his mother passed away. What now? It was a more profound question this time, (no less painful), but more painful if you know what I mean. This was "Mama." It's something totally different when it's "Mama" and not just a sibling or someone else. It's a whole new, different experience. Painful never the less because you love them both, but painful in a different way because it's "Mama." You may have other siblings but you only have one "Mama." At this time my brothers and sisters was still living so I shared with him, "we do what's necessary." Whatever you think is needed at this time, that's what's, "what now?"

Living can be a challenge after all the arrangements has been made, the service attended, everyone gone home to their respected places of residence. Only one more hurdle as far as the departed is concerned. Dealing with the disposal of your loved ones possessions. I think the sooner you do this, the better. Others may not feel this way. They may want to hold on to the possessions because it makes them feel close to their loved one or they just want to hold onto stuff for whatever reason. Not me. I'm the "keep it moving person." Don't get me wrong, there are some keepsakes that I have and also I have loads of pictures. I was always the one taking pictures and keeping them. So I have pictures of all the family and gatherings. But I do want to "keep it moving." They have been laid to rest. They have finished their course, they have run the race. This part of life for them is no more. No sense in me dwelling on that. Making myself miserable and depressed. That's what will happen if you don't move on.

Reality has a way of setting in as time passes. At first you are sort of numb as you go through the process and when all is done, when everyone goes to their different addresses, when the phone stops ringing, when neighbors no longer offer "if you need anything," you begin to realize just how real this is. You began to realize they really are gone. They are not just somewhere for a visit or on vacation; they are GONE, and never coming back. A hard pill to swallow, a jolt back to reality from a bad dream. A rude awakening. My Lord, help! I need you more than ever now. This is a totally different pain now, the realization they are never coming back. The harsh reality that you will never talk to them again, never see them again, never, never, never nothing ever again with them. This can be a very hard place to be. But, thanks be to God who always comforts and consoles.

That's why it is so important to have a relationship with the Lord. To know what His word says about the situation. I personally would not have liked to go through any loss without the Lord. I just can't imagine going through without "Him." It's hard enough to go through with Him but without "Him?" Makes me shudder and I don't even want to think about that. I don't know how some people do it. Wait, yes I do. They don't. They really don't know how to deal with the death of a loved one without Jesus. They try to make you think they are alright; I'm dealing with it they say; I have my bad days and my good days, they say; I only miss them at a certain time they say. All the while smoking a pack of cigarettes (while talking to you); or reaching for the next drink, or some people eat food excessively, some turn to drugs, just to ease the pain, they say. Some people become work alcoholics. Never getting rest until their bodies give out on them.

That's why it's so important to have Jesus as your Savior, your comforter, your best friend, your peace. Oh how we need Jesus, He is our source. No matter what we are going through, He has already been through it all and knows just how you feel. He is the only one that can carry you through at this time. Let Him. He is willing and He is able, He wants to do it for you.

He wants us to be comforted, at peace and full of joy. As He comforts us and we grow in that place of comfort we can then comfort others just as God comforts us. (2 Corinthians 1:3-5) Earth has no sorrow that heaven cannot heal. (Your days of grieving are over.) Isaiah 60:20b, Message Bible

Friends:

There are times when the circle of friends is broken also. As I said, I have learned that death is a part of life. It's not meant to consume or control us it's just part of this journey we call life. I heard someone say, "It's a debt we all have to pay." Hebrews 9:27 says everyone has to die once, then face the consequences (Msg). So as surely as you are born you will follow the order of life and die as everyone does eventually.

God is in charge of that and it's up to you how you choose to live while here.

I have had many friends pass away to eternal rest. One that is very clear and had a profound effect on me was a very dear friend. We would go fishing, near and far. It was never a time she didn't want to go and that was fine with me. We both loved to fish. She would always share her testimony about how God healed her of cancer. Great woman of God. Loved her dearly. To my surprise one day she shared with me that she had not been feeling well and was going to the doctor for test. She did. The diagnosis was not good. But we had the faith of a grain of a mustard seed. Just as God had healed her before, He would do it again. How we prayed. How we fasted. How we trusted God. (Still do) She seemed to be going in the opposite direction of healing but still we believed. We exercised our faith and spoke and read scriptures of healing. Just trusting God every day. Soon she had to be hospitalized. Still I believed God would heal her. For surely as the word declares, "By His stripes, she is healed." And other healing scriptures. I stood on the Word, I believed with all my heart my friend was going to miraculously be raised from that sick bed and we would be traveling and fishing again. I decided to travel to Louisiana (home), for she seemed to be doing better. That was a great relief, she even ate a little food. So I went home for a few days praising the Lord that she was on the road to recovery. No one told me that (medically), I just believed what the Word of God says. I stayed a few days at home and as I didn't get a phone call, so I figured no news was good news. So I headed on back home, had made it almost here to Humble when the call came and I was told my friend had died. I was stunned, to say the least. That could not be possible because God was healing her physical body. He said so in His Word. He is not a man that He should lie, nor the son of man that He should repent: Hath He said, and will He not do it? Or hath He spoken, and will He not make it good. (Numbers 23:19) (ASV) I was very young in the faith back then and I just believed the Word of God literally. I mean, the Word said it and I just knew it was going to happen just like I expected. I could hardly drive on home as by now, the tears are flowing after the initial shock. She can't be gone, I kept telling myself. Then I began to question God. Why? What happened? Your Word said. Why didn't you heal her, you promised in your Word? I now know that God let me rant and rave like that and then He calmly spoke to me and assured me that He did heal her. I'm a little slow and didn't get what He said or what He meant. Part of it was my emotional mindset. So He said again, very clearly, "I did heal her, I just didn't do it the way you wanted me to." That threw me for a loop. What do you mean God, to me, healing is healing and dying is dying. How could she be healed and dead at the same time? I was not understanding. But God is such a great teacher and so strategic in all His ways. I made it home safely, thanks to Him (God). Lord, still couldn't believe it. My husband asked if I'm okay and I say yes (even though I'm not). As time went on the Lord began to minister to me about healing, about other people's will and about being specific in prayer. All of these play a part in healing and it's not always the way we think it should be. God knows each of us and He knows what each of us can bear and He deals accordingly. My friend was tired, her physical body was literally worn out and couldn't take any more of the stress and strain it was going through. She was ready to go home and be with Her Savior. That's what she did. Scripture tells us to be absent in this body is to be present with the Lord (2 Corinthians 5:8). She was ready. She had run her course, she had fought the good fight of faith and was ready to be with the Lord. Once I understood, I couldn't be mad at her. I could only miss her, be glad for her (no more suffering, no more pain, no more sorrow) and thank God that He gave me comfort in understanding. He healed her by taking her home to be with the Lord.

There have been others that passed away and I am very sorry to hear it but some impacted me more than others. One lady had been on oxygen since before I met her and had a serious illness. She was such an inspiration, always sharing the Word and encouraging others. She was always happy even when you knew it was hard for her to breathe. She was such an inspiration and a testimony. She too went home a few years later.

As I said there have been a good many that I was pretty close to, but they were older some of them and some not so old. The older ones I always said, they lived a good long life. The younger ones my heart went out to their families. I felt they hadn't yet lived life fully. But I realize who am I to say whether they did or not.

There was a young lady that used to come to the Senior Center where we would go and have Bible study. We became pretty attached to each other. She had moved here from out of state and she finally told us she was on the donor list waiting for a heart. She was in her late twenties. Beautiful woman of God. One day we were told she was taken to the hospital and she too went home to be with the Lord.

So many young people, it seems. By young I mean they were younger than me. Once again, when I hear of the death of a friend or loved one, I can only depend on and thank God to be God in my life once again and carry me through.

As always He gives me the strength to comfort others, to say the right thing, to just be there to serve or to listen. To give a hug, to encourage. God knows what each of us need and who He wants to minister to the individual.

As we all have, some of my in-laws have passed away. That was tough also as they are just like family. Thanks be to God He does what He do best and make all things possible. Yes, even the death of a loved one.

These past three to four years seem to have been filled with people leaving this earth. Some very close friends that were mother figures to me.

My step-mother was one. I had just talked to her that Sunday morning. We could really talk about nothing and then about everything, especially when it came to the Lord. She had some health challenges but she was doing fine. Nothing major going on, just some test the next day. She had buried some love ones in her day and I admired how she handled herself during those times. The death of two sons, two husbands, mother and father and others that I don't know about. I asked her once (when her baby boy, my baby brother passed away) how she could be that calm. She had a peace that I surely didn't understand. At that time, I did not know Jesus and was running away from Him pretty hard. I thought something was wrong with her because she wasn't acting like how I thought someone should act whose child has died. I kind of thought something was wrong with her. Little did I know she was fine. It was us who wasn't fine. Well certainly not me, didn't have a clue. My baby brother just died and to me that was traumatic. But not her, she had Jesus and she had the peace of God, that comes from knowing and having a relationship with him. I didn't know that then, but I do now.

Later on when I gave my heart to Jesus and begun to grow we developed a beautiful relationship. We would talk for hours. Yes, we even talked about my brother and how she could be that calm and at peace. I know it hurt, I could see and tell that, but the relationship she had with God and her trust in the Lord was something to behold.

My sister called me early the next morning and asked had I heard that she had passed away. I'm so goofy, when someone say, that caused my response is, "girl you shouldn't say things like that cause (Ms. Mae Ola) ain't dead. I was just talking to her yesterday evening." Shock! It was true. I got off the phone with her and began to make calls. Sure enough it was true. I was heartbroken once again. Not down and out, not being able to function, but hurt that a lady I loved like a mother was gone.

I can only thank God for her life and all she taught and imparted to me. I learned a lot from her. Admired her greatly. She was truly one of the great Women of God that has touched my life and impacted, and imparted into my life.

She had already prepared everything for her home going celebration, all the way down to the program. Everything was done. All my brother and sister had to do was carry out her wishes. She had done everything.

The lesson or one of the lessons I learned from that was we all need to prepare for that day. Don't let it be a hardship on your family. They have pre-arranged services that can be paid on monthly or however you choose to do it. But please, get insurance coverage and let it not be a hardship on those that are left. You don't have to go as far as planning the service but by all means have insurance or a pre-arranged service package. It's hard enough to try and make arrangements but not to have the finances for services makes it even harder. I have begun to encourage everyone I know to take this step and prepare for that day that is surely to come. Prepare and plan!

There have been many that have gone home to be with the Lord since then. I've had first cousins and second cousins that have departed. Too many cousins to mention all of them. I'm close with all my relatives.

One dear lady moved here from Oklahoma. Such a beautiful spirited lady. She was always busy. If you were around her she made you feel like you were lazy. She loved to sew and cook. She was very good at both of those. She worked diligently in the church. In Mission, she was always ready to do whatever we were doing all the way down to cooking food. She came up with great ideas that we could do to help the elderly in the nursing homes and even those member's that were homebound. We would be discussing and planning things to do and she would have gone home and already done it. We all always got some "pinto beans and soup." She said, "you can always use soup and pinto beans." They were good too. That sister could cook. We made all kinds of craft items she knew would aid people in wheel chairs and even for our choir. She sewed the majority of the items. So talented and giving. Loved her dearly. Such a sweetheart.

One year her son gave her a limo ride through the city and then out to supper. She could invite three of her friends. I was honored to be one of them. That was a glorious day. We all enjoyed ourselves and she said it was one of the best birthday's she had ever had. The sight-seeing was great and the food was even better. Could never thank her enough for including me. She always called me her baby. Said I was a special person. Always doing things for others. She would give me cards of encouragement and sometimes she would put a little money in the card, just to buy those babies some milk, she would say. (I had my three nieces and a nephew at the time). She would know just when to call and say hello. Just when I needed a pick me up. She was so very dear to me and others. I know her family misses her terribly. I know I do, even now. But I thank God for beautiful memories and great friendships.

Recently another dear friend departed this life also. Same year as my brother went home (the second one). She was another that was like a mother to me. She came to Texas the same year that we moved here. She also was so very special to many people. I had gone to church one Sunday and she was one of the first smiles I saw. She welcomed me with a big hug and made me feel right at home. We joined that church and our journey together began. She was a great teacher, as well as mentor for the younger ladies. She helped me in my spiritual walk more than anyone knows. She was always pushing me, encouraging me, and loving me as a Mother. I remember when she encouraged me to teach Sunday school. I asked her "how she knew I could teach Sunday school?" She said in that deep contralto voice, "Oh you study, you read and you love the Lord, you can do it." She was right. With her help and guidance and through the power of the Holy Spirit, I became a Sunday school teacher. I would call her when I needed clarity on something and she had a way of explaining that made it plain as day. She was a wealth of knowledge. We would study together. We even took some classes together. We became good friends. She was one of my closest friends. Always there when I needed a listening ear or just to listen to me go on and on about nothing. She loved to eat fish and I loved to catch fish. So I even talked her into going fishing with me sometimes. She was very active for her age. I remember we sometimes went to this place fishing I heard about and she and I took off. She would be trying to coax the worm on the hook. I laughed at her real hard. That was so funny. She was talking to the worm saying, "it ain't gone hurt much, just be still." I'm still laughing at her. I told her to squeeze the thing tight and just stick it. She was like, "poor bait." I was like, "you want to catch fish or not." I would end up baiting her hook for her. One time we went and there was a homeless guy there. He talked with us the whole time we were trying to fish. He lived in his car. He had taken out the passenger seat and back seat and made him a bed. Didn't look too comfortable. He told us some tall tales that we knew wasn't true. We both felt sorry for him. Stopped fishing, went to our homes, got some bed linen, comforters, pillows and can goods and took it back to the lake to him. He was so grateful. Don't think anybody had been kind to him in a long time. When we left I told her, we were going to have to be more careful. Nobody knew we were in those woods fishing. She said, "Baby, the Lord got us." I said, "yes ma'am" but purposed to be a little more cautious with strangers. That was just one of the many things we did.

She really encouraged me to discipline myself. She was diagnosed as a diabetic. She would eat what she was supposed to, go for walks she and her husband, every morning. She had that portion control down pat and she pretty much stuck to it. Sometimes I would entice her to have a tiny piece of cake or something. She did what she needed to do, she and her husband took care of themselves. Then she would travel every month to visit with her husband's aunt. She would do all the things that her aunt wouldn't let anyone else do. She always sounded so happy because she was always helping someone else. Then she would go see her mother. Her mother was just as active as her but was beginning to have health challenges. She was always on the go helping somebody.

Such an inspiration and an example to us younger people. She truly taught the younger women and was the example for us as the bible says.

She was so much to so many people. She was to me a mother figure, a mentor, a prayer partner, a teacher, a friend. She always gave of herself until she couldn't give anymore.

When she became ill, I would tell her, "Now it's time for you to let someone do for you." She said, "no baby, I'm alright." She never asked for anything. I would go over and just sit and talk with her. We had some good visits and great talks. We also prayed a lot. She was always thinking of someone else.

I walked through the illness with her for many months, maybe a couple of years, I'm not sure. I'm just glad, once and again, God allowed me to spend time with my friend. In the hospital, the nursing facility, in her home. I appreciate her husband for allowing me to be there all the time. It is such a comfort now to have been able to spend that time with her. I always expected her to bounce back, but the illness began to take its toll on her physical body. She grew tired. I had the opportunity to visit her when she was placed in hospice. I went in, the nurse had said she wasn't responding and didn't know anyone. I went in, talked to her, prayed and I even sang an old hymn. She rolled he head over and looked at me. I knew she recognized me. I asked if she was tired, a tear rolled down her face. I remember she had taught us a class once about your loved one being ill and they were critical and nothing could be done. She told us that we have to release people. She said that it is very selfish of us to hold onto our loved ones as a machine is keeping them alive, or they are in a coma, or the doctor has said there is nothing more they can do. She said, "We need to let people go." That is not living, how they are and they are suffering because we don't want to lose them. I remembered that day, and for me, my part in her life, I said see you later. I released the hold I had on her if any. I prayed, asked God for peace for her, strength for us and that if she was ready, she go peaceably. That's exactly what she did.

I was in Louisiana when her husband called that morning and told me she was gone.

I can't say I wasn't saddened, I was very hurt. But it was also like a release. She wasn't suffering anymore. She was in the presence of the Lord. I was happy for her because she was ready. My girl, my friend, my mentor, spiritual mother. Miss the lady dearly but I feel she is at rest. I could rejoice because I know she is home with the Lord.

Been some months since I've picked up pen and paper. Haven't had the heart, motivation or strength to begin to write again. I have been functioning and doing different things. Life goes on whether we participate or not. Death goes on whether we participate or not. We are not asked whether we want to participate. One day it just shows up on our doorstep (death) and we deal with it or it will deal with us. We will find our self in a cold lonely place. Saddened, mourning and always asking, "Why Lord?" It doesn't have to be this way. We do grieve, we do hurt, and we do mourn. The word declares that blessed are they that mourn for they shall be comforted. We even miss our loved ones more than we think at times than we can bear. But God! We all have loved ones that have departed in one fashion or another. No matter how the transition took place it is still a painful, hurting thing. It can be very devastating, if we allow it to be. The Holy Spirit is a comforter like no other that I know. Friends, family, brother's, sister's, husbands, wives, even mothers can't comfort like the Holy Spirit. Through the Word of God and the presence of the Holy Spirit, it is possible to endure. To move on in life. To function fully in your purpose. No matter the circumstances we face, God is still in control and will act according to His eternal plan. Isaiah 30:18 tells us the Lord is a God of justice for those who wait on Him. He will not abandon us in our time of sorrow (helpless). We must trust that He is able to change the worst situation into a time of hope and joy.

God wants us to see Him as our only hope. Through the pain God will show us that He cares for each of us personally. Don't give up on God. This is not the time to abandon your faith in God. You must continue to trust Him, with all your heart, surrender the faith in you so you can tap into God's divine power. In that place of your pain, the Lord is shaping your heart. He is drawing you closer than ever before to Him and in Him. You are decreasing and He is increasing. No experience should ever be wasted, no matter what it is, be it death, divorce, lay off on a job, sickness, it's still an experience where we can allow to become a landmark and not a stumbling block.

Pain can be a powerful teacher because it forces us to understand that change and struggle are necessary to mature in Christ. Sometimes it seems our lives get worse in situations but God wants to show us He is our only hope. If we can control something on our own, we will never come to know the greater power of God. God loves to prove His faithfulness to us.

You may have had to suffer grief in all kinds of trials. These have come so that the proven genuineness of your faith… may result in praise, glory and honor when Jesus Christ is revealed. 1 Peter 1:6-7

The disciples were with Jesus on a boat crossing the Sea of Galilee; when a furious squall came up, the disciples among them some seasoned fishermen – were afraid for their lives

(Mark 4:37-38). Did God not care? Weren't they handpicked by Jesus and closest to Him? Weren't they obeying Jesus who told them to "Go over to the other side?" (Verse 35) Why then, were they going through such a turbulent time?

No one is exempt from the storms of life. Storms we face can bring us to a deeper knowledge of God. As we are on this journey with Jesus, we learn that no storm is big enough to prevent God from accomplishing His will. (Mark 5:1) Not even the storm of death can stop us from leaning and depending on Jesus, our anchor in any storm.

We can always depend on God to comfort us. Through Isaiah, God told the Israelites, "As a mother comforts her child, so I will comfort you." Isaiah 66:13 God promises to give His children peace and carry them the way a mother carries a child on her hip. God's ability and desire to comfort His people can also be found in the book of 2 Corinthians 1:3-4. He is the one who comforts us in all our troubles. God is gentle, sympathetic, and compassionate when we are mourning or any other trouble we may be experiencing. He is also so very patient with us. He understands and allows us to have our "moments." Then He picks us up and comforts as only He can. If we let Him. As I have said before, we have to let Him, He wants to, but we have to be willing and want to come out of that place of sorrow. We have to ask God to help us and know that nothing separates us from His love. He assures us of His care for us through the power of the Holy Spirit. God always comforts His people (He promises). If you let Him – He will do it.

Cast all your cares upon Him, for He cares for you. (1 Peter 5:7) No matter how your flesh feels, cast all your sorrows on Him. Whenever death comes. He can handle it. Nothing, not even death is too small for Him to care or too big for Him to handle. Humble yourself before God. (1 Peter 5:6) Trust in the Lord with all your heart, lean not to your own understanding, but in all your ways acknowledge Him and He will direct your path. (Proverbs 3:5-6) Keep your thoughts focused on the Lord. Stay in the Spirit. Walk in the Spirit, that you don't fulfill the lust of the flesh. Gal. 5:16. Keep your mind stayed on Jesus and He will keep you in perfect peace. Isaiah 26:3. As your mind wanders sometimes and want to take you back to that place of sorrow, put on some praise music, began to talk to God, began to tell the Lord how you are feeling. He already knows, just want you to acknowledge your feelings. It's not wrong to remember your loved one. You will always remember them. They were a part of your life. No matter what the relationship was, they were your loved ones. Remember the good times, the happiness you built together. The joy you bought to your love one. The joy they bought to and shared in your life. Remember! Memories are good. Just don't pull up and park there. You are in a new season. Another phase has begun for you.

Do not use negative words. Speak positive words that agree with the Word of God. There is power in our tongue. Life and death is in the power of the tongue. Proverbs 21:16 When you speak negative words, you give voice to the thoughts of the enemy. He will definitely use them against you too. Try to make you think, "If only." If only I had did this. If only I had done that, if only I would have been there. If only, if only, if only. Don't let the enemy play with your mind. It's just as easy to say and agree with the Word of God as it is to say the negative. So take the energy you have and use it to confess the Word of God. Speak faith words. Declare what the Word says.

Psalm 91:2 says, "I will say of the Lord, He is my refuge and my fortress; my God; in Him will I trust." Trust the

Lord, He is willing and able to bring you out of despair into a place of peace and joy beyond your understanding.

Mark 11:23 declares that whoever says to this mountain. Be removed and cast into the sea; and does not doubt in His heart, but believes that those things he says will be done, he will have whatever he says. Go give it to God. Find faith filled scriptures and began to declare and stand on the Word, believing that what so ever you confess you have it. Psalm 62:8 tells us to trust in Him at all times, ye people, pour out your heart before Him: God is a refuge for us. Selah. (Pause and calmly think on that)

Find scriptures that speak to your heart and brings you comfort. There are so many promises from God and He keeps them all.

John 11:33 is a great promise that I personally love. "These things I have spoken unto you, that in me you might have peace. In the world you shall have tribulations, but be of good cheer; I have overcome the world. No matter what we face we can take comfort in knowing that Christ has overcome it all. We understand we are not exempt from tribulations (whatever it may be) but we have the peace of God and His promise that we can overcome any situation.

Jesus tells us in John 14:27, Peace I leave with you, my peace I give unto you, not as the world giveth, give I unto you. John 14:1 Let not your heart be troubled, neither let it be afraid. In the time of the passing of a loved one, there is no jewel as precious as peace. Its right up there with comfort and no one does it as well as Jesus. Grab a hold of that peace and don't let nothing snatch it away from you. Let it become your life support.

The strength that God provides is almost unreal. You may not think you can go on or you can't do the next necessary step. But I promise, the strength God gives carries you to that place in the super natural causing you to do what is needed even though you may have thought you couldn't. He tells us to Fear thou not; for I am with thee; be not dismayed; for I am thy God. I will strengthen thee; yea, I will help thee; yea, I will uphold thee with the right hand of my righteousness. Isaiah 41:14

The strength of the Almighty, just like His peace, passes all our understanding and comprehension. He is faithful. He meets our every need in every challenge we face in life. Nothing takes Him by surprise so He already has the solution. We depend on Him the more to take us through the valley of the shadow of death. We don't have to fear no evil because He is with us. Psalm 23:4. The entire number of Psalm 23 is an excellent source of comfort. He promises to never leave us or forsake us. He is always there. He is always there. Hebrews 13:5

I lean heavily on the Word of God. On the comfort of friends, the kind words of even strangers. Even those God would use to share an experience. They may not even know how it has touched you this day. But He knew what you needed and provided it. That's just the way our God is.

I have heard of other's that have gone through or is going through the transition of a loved one departing this life. I know I am not the only one who has had numerous love ones that are gone. I know their loved ones was and still is just as precious to them as mine are to me. I sympathize with each one. Those I know of and those that I don't personally know. No experience is the same. The act may be the same but the experience is oh so different for each of us. But we can relate in our special way. There is a common bond that says I understand, I'm here for you or just a phone call and comforting words.

Once again, it has been a minute since I have picked up pen and paper. Sorta got in a habit of not doing it, writing. Even though on every hand I hear, write that book. At prayer service, the intercessor prayed for author's to write that book. At church, the pastor encouraged if you are called to write a book, write that book, at ladies meetings where no one but God knows you from Adam, somehow manages to say, in her message, "whatever you are called to do, if it's to write a book, write that book." All you hear it seems is "write that book." I'm always encouraged and say to myself. I'm going to finished what I started. But …, Do you know that but cancels out whatever you said before. Just a little side note.

The but for me is a while after my baby sister and my friends, a few others I knew had gone home to be with the Lord, I was just a little sick of death. Just a little bit, but sick of it none the less. Like I'm in control of something; so I didn't get started right away. Talked to the Lord about how tired I am of people dying. He didn't mind my talking to Him about it, He already knew my thoughts anyway.

A publishing company called one day. He was very encouraging and he asked questions. I shared that I wasn't sure I was going to do the book since I had pretty much stopped writing. I said there are plenty of books on the subject that I'm writing about and he pretty much said what the Lord had said. "There may be plenty of books on the subject, but not by me." Not my story. I said to myself "whoa, that is what He, God said." I have to agree. My story is my story and someone else is theirs. I don't know who this book will be used to help, someone that God knows needs it.

My sister's and I talk a lot. We really missed those that had gone on. Two sisters and a brother from my mother. My younger sister began to have health challenges. Had to have surgery. She was very close to our baby sister. If a person didn't know better, they would think they were twins. They looked nothing alike, but had a bond that was very close. We all had that but she was really closer to her. Her no longer being here really did something to her. She was not handling it very well at all. She tried to make me think she was okay. We all talked about them and how much we missed them, but when she talked it was something more. I would say girl, we sure do miss ole Calla Belle. My pet name for her. She told me she talked to her all the time. I said, "Really." Would try to play it off, like, girl, we don't talk to dead people. They are no longer here. She would say, yeah I know. She was grieving really hard and there was nothing I could do about it, except share the Word of God. That's what helped me. And it always helped me to be able to talk to them, the ones that were left. Get together, enjoy each other's company and remember the time we had with each other. Somehow, I could tell that just wasn't enough for her. She really, really missed her baby sister. She missed the rest, but she really missed her so much. Seems she just didn't want to go on without her. She went through the motions of daily life but, she just missed her sister so much. She would even tell me at times that her sister came to visit, her. She was grieving hard. As long as I talked to her and encouraged her, we'd talk about the Word and she seemed fine. Then I would talk to one of the others and they too would notice her whole conversation was about her baby sister and how they had these talks. Lord have mercy. She began to complain of stomach problems. Had already had one surgery and came through that just fine. God healed her of that and she seemed to mend well and was even bouncing back and enjoying everyday life. Her children and grand-children even her friends. But she still complained of her stomach not being right and she was in a lot of pain. She was finally hospitalized and they diagnosed her with one thing. Released her, she seemed to be better, she couldn't hardly eat anything or had a desire for food. I shared with her one day, I said, girl, "You really are grieving for Carrie huh?" She said she missed her but she was alright. I went and visited with her and stayed almost the whole week. She had lost a lot of weight, I noticed. I encouraged her to eat more and she just said her stomach hurt real bad whenever she did eat. She had had a light stroke earlier on and was doing therapy for that. We enjoyed the visit with each other. As I said, I am the oldest girl, so it was like I was mother hen. Took care of her while I was there and just enjoyed her company.

Wasn't long after that they took her to the hospital and they ran test after test only to say one thing, not really knowing at all what was going on. I made it my business to go and see for myself what was going on and to try to get an answer and some kind of understanding of the overall situation. My sister was very ill. More so than anyone had told me. They finally told me she had a hole in her small intestine. She has always been diabetic and now this. They were going to treat her some kind of way that would cause the pin hole to close up. Only thing with that was the liquid food they gave her ran her insulin level up real high. She also did dialysis three times a week. We prayed and trusted God. The liquids only seemed to help, so they were to continue that routine. They moved her to another facility where they were better equipped for that. The doctor said she was a very sick woman. Tell me something I didn't know! Anyway my God is the God that can do the exceeding abundant above all that I could ask or even think. (Eph. 3:20) I stayed the week there. Glad I could spend that time with her. They had her heavily sedated because of the pain she was in. In her waking moments we would talk and laugh. I had my I-pod, so I would play us music. She liked the old gospel songs but we listened to all kinds of Christian music, played healing CD's and just saturated the atmosphere with the presence of God.

She was still in pain and sedated but I thought she was getting better. I told her that night that I was going home the next day. She said, "Don't leave me." I jokingly told her, girl I been here a whole week, got to go see about my folks. She seemed to be better. I went on down to my home town which is seventy one miles away. My nieces and sister was going up there to visit with her so I turned around and went back with them. Glad I did. We had a good visit. All of us there. Her children, grand-children, my nieces (hers too) and other sister. She slept most of the time because of the medication. I came on back home after the visit. Was really concerned about her. Something wasn't right. I prayed as usual and trusting God is all I got. He always has the final say. So I stand on that, trusting that He will heal my sister, raise her up with a testimony and make her whole. You can do it God! You can do anything but fail. You are a faithful God and if I ask anything according to your will, you hear me and you answer me. I prayed. I believed. I still do believe even more so now than ever before. And He has never, failed me. Or you. He is a good God – watching over His Word to perform it. But, He knows what's best and even though it may not look like it at the time. He makes all things work together for our good. He always does.

Hadn't been home a day. Called later that evening to check on her. Her daughter was there and I was talking to her. She began to scream and tell me, "Mama coding." I began to pray. I told her your mama ain't coding, I just left there. She was hysterical and I was trying not to accept what she said, but sadly it was true. They got her stabilized and moved her into the ICU unit. I called my niece and told her to go up there and see for me what was going on. Meanwhile her daughter was saying they said it didn't look good. I'm telling her and praying, "We got to trust God, he has the final say." Throughout all the challenges I have faced with the home going of my brothers and sisters, I still trusted God to raise her and them up, each time. I always had hope that they would live and not die and declare the works of the Lord. But again, I'm just Rosemary and He is God, who knows what's best. He knows what tomorrow holds, He knows our every thoughts and the plans He has for each of us. He even honors our will. We do have a will.

Most of the time my will is not someone else's will. So we have to accept when a person exercise their will to go and be with the Father and leave us behind. At this point it's not about you or me, it's their will that God honors. It hurts us and grieves us, but in the end it's their right as a believer to go and be with the Lord. No matter how we may feel. Paul said in Philippians 1:23, I am hard pressed between the two, I desire to depart and be with Christ, which is better by for, so it is a person's right and will to choose to go home with the Father.

Sometimes that really is what's best and it is for the good for all concerned (except the family of the individual). They truly don't understand and don't want to understand that their love one no longer being here is the best thing. I remember a time when that is exactly what happened. A friend, a very dear friend became ill, we all believed that person would be raised up and God would be glorified through this miraculous occurrence. We even had a "Word" from the Lord that the individual would live and not die to declare the works of the Lord. We trusted the Word of God. We believed literally that was what was happening. I keep remembering that our thoughts are not God's thoughts, His ways are so much higher than ours. It definitely didn't happen as we believed. Not in the way we thought anyway. Our friend went home to be with the Lord. We were all devastated, cause that was not the way we thought it should happen. Later my friend told me that the Lord said if she could release him to God she would see him (her husband live and not die). I was still trying to comprehend that the person had died. I was still kinda young in the faith, but I believed, if you know what I mean. It was explained to me that because of that one person's death, many got a chance to live. You see, the individual impacted a lot of lives. They gave their lives to Jesus because of the witness of this one person. There was not just one person but many gave their lives to God. So the greater good came because He made a choice to be with the Lord and let his life be a great witness. So with that being said, all we can do is accept the situation and continue to trust God. He can use all instances for the good of those that love Him and are called according to His purpose. They have finished their course, they have kept the faith and when the time came they finished their course. 2 Timothy 4:6-7. God honor's their will and He always knows what's best.

I continued to talk to my family back home. Different ones was saying different things. I trusted my niece to get the full details and no matter it didn't look or feel good for my sister. They said technically she was gone but the machine was breathing for her, no brain activity, kidney's not functioning and so on. Just a bad report. They made the decision to take her off the ventilator. I made the decision to continue to trust God and continue to pray. He always has the final say. So I went down on my knees with the latest news I had received and I once again prayed for healing for my sister. This could not be true that she was technically gone. God you can do anything I cried out. Nothing is too hard for you, you are the giver of life. Then it seems as if a peace came over me and God allowed me to remember all she had been enduring these past months, all that she was dealing with now. Her trials, her tribulations, her sorrows and her pain. He said, "She's tired." Of course I wanted to argue with God, "How can she be tired, she got you, you the one with all power. She can't get tired, help her Lord. Please, help her. But just as I said all that, I felt my shoulder's slump as if I had been tensed up, I felt a release in the Spirit and I remember saying, "Never the less Lord, not my will but your will be done." Help me Lord. I had said that only a moment ago, when the phone rang, I believe I was when getting off my knees when my husband came in and said, "She's gone." I already knew of course. It was as if when I said, not my will but yours be done was the moment I released yet another sister. Lord, Lord, Lord.

Wow! That's all I can say is "Wow." Didn't want to believe it. I was here in Humble and they were there in Louisiana. Really wished I could have been with the rest of the family at this time, but again, God knows what is best. I really am thankful that I wasn't there.

We handled business. Did what had to be done. It was if I was going through the motions once again after the other three. All I can say is, God is a keeper. He kept me and the rest of the family once again, as He always does. He is so faithful.

It's never an easy task to say good-bye to a love one. My sister and I would always say, "See you later" when we would leave each other, never good-bye. So I said, "See you later" to my sister and leaned on God harder than ever. I thank Him for all those who had kind words, checked on us, did all the things you are supposed to do at this time.

We had a beautiful home-going celebration for her of course. I couldn't help but think, just some months earlier she and I had been viewing the body of our baby sister, before that, our older brother, before that our baby brother. Now I was viewing her all by myself. Jesus! Oh sweet Jesus. All I can say is God is faithful. I felt His presence like never before. Even though my flesh felt like it was in the valley of the shadow of death, my God was there with me. And He has always been there ever since. I know that those can sound like just words, but there is a measure of comfort in knowing, He never leaves me, nor forsakes me. He is my comforter. When I'm at my lowest, when I miss one of them beyond my wildest dreams, He comforts me as I cry out to Him.

Even as I write, the memories are so very fresh and hurtful, but God. Thank God we are not moved by what we feel but we walk by faith. My faith has and still is sustaining me. Keeping me in perfect peace as I keep my mind stayed on Him (Jesus Christ).

Yes, I have my moments. Yes, I miss them terribly. I can be doing something as simple as washing dishes and an overwhelming desire for them comes over me, and I say Lord, I miss my sister, or my brother. Sometimes takes me a minute to come from that place of missing them, but God always bring me back. Thank you Lord for not letting me stay over there in that place of despair.

It's okay to miss them. It's okay to remember. For me just not good to get in that place of hopelessness, wishing that things could be different or what if this had happened! Not good! Time to praise the Lord for His comforting ministry of the Holy Spirit.

Since the home-going of my sisters and brothers, many others have gone on also. Some I knew personally and others were people I knew in general, I always try to share the Word of God with the ones I talk to, knowing at the time, it's just that, Words. You know the Word and you believe the Word, but I've found out, that you have to become the Word. You have to live it, be it and it will carry you through the darkest valley.

I've also learned along the way that life is going through one loss after another, one crisis after another, one challenge after another. Life is made up of all these things. As I said before, death is a part of life. You cannot get around or away from it, just like all the challenges that come. But you can embrace it. Embrace the situation and let God get the glory out of the situation. You be built up and develop a closer relationship with God.

It's how you allow God to teach you to embrace such moments and times when grief or other circumstances happen. We have to learn to receive the true healing that comes only from God. This true healing comes from and through God as we allow Him to bring us through this process at this time in our lives.

Each person's response to grief and death is unique in and of itself. It's your experience. Doesn't matter what others know or feel, they cannot truly know what you feel. Only God knows how you feel and what you are dealing with. They can sympathize with you but your experience is your experience. Yes, others have had similar experience but yours is yours. Each ones experience is different, you react different. It's a personal thing and you deal with it accordingly.

Not only is your dealing with your grief your own personal experience, know in your heart that it's just as personal to God. He knows exactly where you are and He is the only one that can identify with what you are going through. There is nothing we go through that He hasn't experienced Himself. Hebrews 4:15 declares, "For we do not have a high priest who is unable to understand and sympathize and have shared a feeling with our weaknesses and infirmities and liability to the assaults of temptation, but one who has been tempted in every respect as we are, yet without sinning (AMP). He is the one to trust your feeling to at a time such as this and everything else you are dealing with. He loves you so much and He knows you intimately and nothing takes Him by surprise. He is not shocked or surprised by anything that concerns you. He knows your way of grieving is distinctly your own and He has the plans to bring you through with all the grace you need to endure. Be strong and take heart, all you who hope in the Lord declares Psalm 31:24.

When you feel at your lowest point, just know and trust in the Lord. When your heart feels as though there will be no mending, trust and hope in the Lord. Our hope is in Him. Our confidence is that He can and will carry us through. Choose to trust Him, choose to hope in Him, choose life and know that you can live again with memories, endurable memories that will be pleasant all because our faith is in Him.

Understand it's a process. Everything we go through even when our loved ones go on home to glory it's still a process to do what needs to be done, a process to attend the home-going services, then the process of living day to day without your loved one. You don't have to rush it, work the process and take it day by day. Let God guide you each day – trust Him on every hand. Although we know and trust the Lord, the Spirit is willing but the flesh is weak (Matthew 26:41). And in our flesh, our emotions (the soulish area) where we still feel the pain and the loss. It's part of life and we learn to manage every area of our life. We learn to trust God's timing for you, His timing, for me, to help us not to allow pain to control our life. He can and will. Continue to ask Him to help you. If you have to ask Him each morning, if you have to ask Him throughout the day, ask Him, "Lord Help me." He wants to help you. There is not a set time when your grieving period is over. I don't think it's ever over or goes away – we learn and allow God to help us deal with it on a daily basis. Just take it one day at a time. God already knows the timing and how it's going. Let Him handle your cares and anxieties and fears or whatever you are dealing with. Let Him be the Comforter that only He can be. We always ask and then try to handle it ourselves. Release it to God so He can be God! Release it to God and receive the peace that passes your understanding that peace that keeps your heart and guards your mind, do what He instructs us to do. Matthew 11:28-29 - Come unto me, all you who labor and are heavy laden and I will give you rest. Take my yoke upon you and learn of me, for I am meek and lowly (AMP). Come to me all who labor and are heavy laden, overburdened I will cause you to rest. (I will ease and relieve and refresh your souls. Verse 29 – Take My yoke upon you and learn of me, for I am gentle (meek), humble (lowly) in heart and I will find rest (relief and ease and refreshment and recreation and blessed quite) for your soul. (Jeremiah 6:16) 30:4 My yoke is wholesome (useful, good-not harsh, hard, sharp or pressing, but comfortable, gracious and pleasant and my burden is light and easy to be borne. By no means will the pain go away, the problems go away, but, Jesus will help you bear them. You are not alone with your grief, He is there, you must call unto Him and then listen. Listen and receive the peace and the rest in Christ. God truly does understand and has compassion for us. Sometimes we may feel as though we are alone in our grief and no one knows what we are going through or dealing with, but He does and He cares. He knows all, sees all, and is all powerful at the same time. Allow your trust and faith to increase as you lean on Him the more. I always say, "Give all your cares to God, go to bed get a good night's sleep, cause He gone be up all night anyway. He never sleep nor slumbers (Psalm 121:4), so you may as well sleep. Sweet sleep. He gives you that too.

During this time it can be a great experience with God. You can experience Him like never before in the deepest realm of your being. That includes any situation you may be dealing with at this moment.

Cast all your cares on Him and experience the freedom from pain, depression, worry anxiety or whatever the case maybe. You can overcome this.

My pastor has written a pamphlet (small book) about death. Very understanding and helpful at a time such as this.

He explains at the end not to isolate yourself. First He says, "Don't blame God," secondly, don't blame others, thirdly, don't blame yourself. Don't allow the enemy the opportunity to play with your mind with all kinds of negative stuff. And lastly stay in fellowship with your church. You have your immediate family but God has also given you an extended family, your church. Continue to be in fellowship with them, continue to be involved in church related activities, most of all, continue to trust God with all your heart, your soul and your mind. May God continue to heal and comfort you as only He, a loving, compassionate, kind, caring God can. And Amen.

CPSIA information can be obtained
at www.ICGtesting.com
Printed in the USA
FFOW02n1728250418
46365453-48036FF